Writing Strands

A COMPLETE WRITING PROGRAM
USING A PROCESS APPROACH
TO WRITING AND COMPOSITION

ASSURING
CONTINUITY AND CONTROL

LEVEL 3

of
a complete writing program
for homeschoolers

a
publication
of

NATIONAL WRITING INSTITUTE
624 W. University #248
Denton, TX 76201-1889

Manufactured in the United States of America

ISBN 1-888344-10-5

For information: Write,   National Writing Institute,
                         624 W. University #248
                         Denton, TX 76201-1889

                         Call,   (800) 688-5375
                         e-mail, info@writingstrands.com

NATIONAL WRITING INSTITUTE PUBLICATIONS

STUDENTS
Writing Strands Level 1
Writing Strands Level 2
Writing Strands Level 3
Writing Strands Level 4
Writing Strands Level 5
Writing Strands Level 6
Writing Strands Level 7
Writing Exposition
Creating Fiction

Communication And Interpersonal Relationships

Dragonslaying Is For Dreamers
Axel Meets The Blue Men
Axel's Challenge

PARENTS/TEACHERS

Evaluating Writing

Reading Strands

Analyzing The Novel:
Dragonslaying Is For Dreamers

INTRODUCTION

This group of exercises in the series called *Writing Strands* is designed to give homeschooled students a grounding in the very complicated process of giving others their thoughts in written form. This level is designed for students who, in public school, would be considered ready for third or even up to seventh grade. Of course, third and seventh grade students would write much differently, but that is not a problem. Both can experience learning the skills presented in this level. It has been designed to be widely applied, and there are many experiences here that most young writers should have.

Learning to write skillfully is one of the hardest jobs that you have. These exercises will make it easier. Much of the planning and detail of the writing process is presented here.

The writing exercises in this level are in four categories: basic, creation, organization, and description. The exercises in each of these areas will guide you in the development of the skills you'll need.

Rather than increase the work for your parents, this writing process should make it easier for both you and your parents to meet the demands for student writing skill.

When these exercises are completed, you will have a well-founded introduction to this most difficult skill, and your parents will find it easier to have confidence that this part of the teaching challenge has been met.

When you finish each writing exercise, if you then spend about a week reading and discussing ideas with your parents, you will have a language arts program that will last you for a full year. If you are a more advanced student doing some catch up or if you want to do two or three days in one day in this book, that's fine, finish sooner.

You should discuss with your parents taking a week off from writing after each exercise. This is what I suggest that you do. This then will mean that you will have one year to complete each level of *Writing Strands*. This is the way this program was designed.

CONTENTS

HOW TO MAKE

WRITING STRANDS WORK FOR YOU

1. You should have a writing folder containing all of your written work which should be kept for your next level. This will give you a place to store and record your skills, and it's a great thing for your parents to have if they have to make a report on your progress.

2. Both semesters' work have evaluations to be made by your parents. They contain:
   a) The objectives you have mastered that semester; and,
   b) A place for them to comment on your work and a place to list the things you have yet to learn.

3. Each exercise begins with a suggested time for completion. Of course, all students work at different rates. The suggested daily activities can be combined or extended depending on your desire and your parents' goals.

4. Many of the exercises suggest that your parents will work with you during your writing period reading what you have written. If this is done, it will serve two purposes:
   a) It will give you constant feedback and will allow your parents to catch many writing problems before they appear in your final papers.
   b) It will greatly cut down on your parents' correcting efforts. Most of the paper reading can be done during your writing time, so, even though you will be writing much more than you previously have been, your parents should be able to help you more using even less time.

5. At the end of each semester's work there is an evaluation form that your parents can use that could list the problems you have yet to solve:
   a) The form at the end of the first semester should contain a listing of the problems that you should work on during the second semester.
   b) The year's-end evaluation form should list the problems that you can solve next year.

6. Your parents might use the book *Evaluating Writing* to help them and you with your writing. If they do, it will help you both a great deal with the development of your skills.

7. It might be good if you don't write in this book at all but use other paper and make copies of those pages at the end of each semester's work where you can list the problems you've solved and the ones at the end of each exercise called "Record of Progress." This way your book will be completely clean for your younger brothers or sisters to use.

PRINCIPLES

The following principles were adopted by National Writing Institute before work began on *Writing Strands*. They were our guides in the initial stages of the design of the exercises.

1. Every person needs to learn to express ideas and feelings in writing.

2. There is no one right way to write anything.

3. The ability to write is not an expression of a body of knowledge that can be learned like a list of vocabulary words.

4. Writing teachers and their students both learn in any effective writing situation.

5. The product of each student's writing efforts must be seen as a success for at least the following reasons:
   a) A student in a writing situation is not in competition with anyone else.
   b) There is no perfect model against which any effort can be compared for evaluation, so there is no best way for any student to write.
   c) Every controlled writing experience will help students improve the ability to express themselves.

6. All student writing efforts are worthy of praise. The most help any writing teacher can give at any point is to show, in a positive way, what is good about a piece and how it might be improved.

7. Any writing lesson assigned, which is done independently by the student and does not have a teacher's constant feedback in the form of reinforcement and suggestions, represents a missed opportunity for the student.

8. All writing at any level is hard work, and every writer should be encouraged to feel the pride of authorship.

9. All young authors need to be published. This can be accomplished by having their work read to other family members, posted on bulletin boards (refrigerators), printed in "books" or read by other family members.

10. Students should learn that writing is fun, exciting and rewarding. This cannot be taught to a student who is punished by being made to write. Punishments, such as writing fifty times "I will not argue with my brothers" will certainly destroy the joy of learning to write.

EXERCISES * SKILL AREAS * OBJECTIVES

Exercise 1: **Following Directions**

Skill Area: Basic

Objectives: 1. Believing that it is possible to follow directions
2. Understanding that it is good to follow directions
3. Understanding what makes a sentence

Exercise 2: **Controlling Sentences And Paragraphs**

Skill Area: Basic

Objectives: 1. Including more than one thing in a sentence
2. Understanding the relationship between main and supporting ideas
3. Writing an organized paragraph

Exercise 3: **Writing And Rewriting A Sentence**

Skill Area: Basic

Objectives: 1. Writing a simple sentence
2. Making a simple sentence more complicated
3. Connecting a number of complicated sentences to make a story

Exercise 4: **My Friend**

Skill Area: Description

Objectives: 1. Organizing what will be described
2. Describing the appearance of a friend
3. Seeking help from your parent
4. Rewriting parts of a paper to improve it

Exercise 5: **What The Storyteller Tells The Reader**

Skill Area: Creation

Objectives: 1. Understanding that characters think when they talk
2. Writing about characters who think

Exercise 6: **"What Did You Do Today?"**

Skill Area: Organization

Objectives: 1 Organizing a description
2. Using experiences to help organize
3. Planning organized answers

Exercise 7: **Furniture**

Skill Area: Organization

Objectives: 1. Examining a number of objects
2. Organizing objects so their placement can be understood

Exercise 8: **Out The Window**

Skill Area: Description

Objectives: 1. Understanding that all people do not see the same things
2. Organizing what is seen
3. Establishing a character's position by telling what that character could see

Exercise 9: **A Very Short Story**

Skill Area: Creation

Objectives: 1. Planning a very short story
2. Writing the parts of a story
3. Putting these parts together

Exercise 10: **My Room**

Skill Area: Description

Objectives: 1. Understanding that the world is an organized place
2. Realizing the need to understand organizations
3. Describing something in an organized way

Exercise 11: **How People Move When They Talk**

Skill Area: Description

Objectives: 1. Punctuating dialogue
2. Describing characters' actions
3. Creating characters who move as they talk

Exercise 12: **Story Events**

Skill Area: Organization

Objectives: 1. Understanding that a story is a series of events
2. Creating a story from a series of events

Exercise 13:   **Tell A Story**

Skill Area: Creation

Objectives: 1. Planning the telling of an event
2. Supplying the details to the event
3. Telling the parts of the event in order
4. Maintaining point of view

Exercise 14:   **Liking The Character**

Skill Area: Creation

Objectives: 1. Understanding that all characters in stories are not liked by all readers
2. Creating characters who will be liked

STRANDS

This writing program has been designed to start with very simple directions to produce very simple writing. You'll find that the work will get much harder as you progress. This is not all bad. You should expect to get better at writing as you practice.

To help you and your parents understand how this progression of difficulty works, we have listed below the strands, the exercises that present the strands and where they are found in this text.

NOT RULES,

MORE LIKE SUGGESTIONS

In almost everything we do, there are rules (like laws), and then there are what we call "rules." The rules that are like laws are written and we all accept these as the rules we have to live by. Then there are the "rules," the things that we *should* do, that we agree to do, and things that make life nicer for everyone if we do them.

This is also true in writing. As an example of the difference in the rules of writing, look at the rule (law) that says that every sentence must start with a capital letter. This is written down and we all must write using this rule. A "rule" of writing is that we use an exclamation point only once a year.

The following "rules" are just strong suggestions. You can violate them if you want to. It might be good to keep in mind however, that if you do, your readers will look at your writing the same way that the company at dinner might look at you if you burped at the end of the meal. So, below is a short list of the "rules" of writing:

1. Don't use exclamation points! This makes any writing look amateurish and fuzzy. If you're saying something that's important, the way you say it should be strong enough so that you don't have to tell your reader that it's important by using exclamation points at the end of your sentences.

2. Don't underline the titles of your papers. The only time there should be an underline in one of your titles is when you use the names of books or magazines.

3. Skip a line after the title in any paper you're giving to someone else to read.

4. Never write *The End* at the end of anything you write for a schooling exercise.

5 Don't try writing humor until you've studied it and really know the difference between being funny and being corny. (Those places in this book where I've tried to be funny and was corny will give you an example of what I mean.)

6. Don't skip a line between paragraphs.

7. Always leave a margin at the bottom of each page.

8. Check your papers for clichés before you write the final drafts.

1 FOLLOWING DIRECTIONS

SKILL: BASIC

It may take you three days to:
1. Believe that it is possible to follow directions
2. Understand that it is good to follow directions
3. Understand what makes a sentence

PREWRITING

Day One:

You may work alone the first two days of this exercise. Your parent may not need to read it to you nor explain it to you. You can do it and do a good job all by yourself. Sometimes it's handy to have someone around to help, but it's not <u>always</u> necessary.

I've heard lots of people tell each other that kids can't follow directions. I never believed this. Did you start reading this page at the bottom? Did you start reading this paragraph at the end? Did you start reading from right to left? Of course you didn't. You followed the directions that you were given years ago about how to read from the left to the right and from the top to the bottom.

This exercise is designed to teach your parents that you *can* follow directions. Sometimes it is important to teach parents things, right? I'm going to give you some directions, and you'll follow them exactly as you should. Then, in the future, when someone tells you that you don't follow directions well, you can answer, "Ah, but I can now. I have learned to do it just exactly right."

Read this paragraph.

A sentence is a statement one person tells another. A question is what one person asks another. They both have to make sense.

Until you're older, there is no such thing as a one-word sentence. Really! Write each statement or question so your reader understands what you're saying or want to know.

> **Hint: Work alone if you can.**

One word is not a sentence. Read that sentence again.

One word is not a sentence.

Sometimes you have to follow directions even when you don't think you're doing so.

Sometimes two words can make a sentence. *Bill ran*. That's a sentence. *Bill*. That's not a sentence. *Ran*. That's not a sentence. A sentence must have two things. A *noun* and a *verb*. You know this and this isn't a grammar lesson. You're following directions, remember?

In our sentence, *Bill ran*, the word, *Bill*, is the noun. A noun is a subject—a person, a place or a thing. Do you know a Bill who is a thing? Most Bills are people. I get and pay the gas bill, but that's something else.

Ran is a verb, a word that shows action. It's what Bill did. It's an action word.

Read this sentence twice. Read this sentence twice.

Sometimes there's no way to avoid following directions, is there?

WRITING

You're to write a two-word sentence. Write it on other paper.

1_____ 2_____

Did you write a two-word sentence? If your two-word sentence starts with *Bill* and ends with *ran*, write one on different paper using different words. If you didn't start with *Bill* and end with *ran*, don't write another sentence.

Wait! Read that paragraph again. You must do exactly what it says. If you're in any doubt about what it means, tap yourself lightly on the nose—and read it again.

1_____ 2_____

If you wrote *Bill ran*, read the paragraph above again. If you wrote a two-word sentence that starts with a person or a place or a thing and ends with an action word, you might have written a good sentence.

Tell your parent that you're at the end of day one. Did you do it? *DO IT*.

> **Hint: Every sentence ends with a period, an exclamation point or a question mark.**

Day Two:

This is an exercise in following directions, remember? You're to add to your two-word sentence that you wrote for day one. If your sentence starts with a person's name, or the label of a person, like Bill or Coach, then your sentence might be a good one.

If your sentence starts with the name of an object, you might be having trouble. *Car ran*. That's not a sentence. *Rain fell*, is a sentence, but that gets complicated.

You'll now write a sentence with three words in it. The third word will explain something to the reader that the reader might want to know, *Bill ran home*, *Dogs chase cats*, or *I poisoned dinner*. There still is a subject and there still is a verb but there's more information. *The third word could be added anywhere in the new sentence.*

On other paper write five sentences. Each one should add information to the one that comes before it. If you don't understand how many sentences you're to write, read this paragraph again. *The new words can be added anywhere to each previous sentence.*

The first sentence should have two words in it. Don't start with *Bill*.

1) _____ _____ _____.

The second sentence should have three words in it.

2) _____ _____ _____.

The third sentence should have four words in it. (Put the new word anywhere.)

3) _____ _____ _____ _____.

The fourth sentence should have five words in it.

4) _____ _____ _____

_____ _____.

The fifth sentence should have six words in it.

5) _____ _____ _____

_____ _____ _____.

> **Hint: Do _exactly_ as the directions tell you.**

Now go back and count the number of words in each of your sentences. If you don't have the right number of words in each of your sentences, erase some or add some.

Day Three:
You have a chance to put to use what you've learned about following sentences and writing directions. . . .Did I get that right? You must know what I mean.

To demonstrate that you understood this exercise, you might find some writing you did some time ago and redo it using what you just learned. Take a paragraph or a page of writing and rewrite it and make the sentences more complicated.

If it works out, be sure and show it to your mom, dad, and anyone else you see. If it's no better that what you wrote before, don't tell people you learned how to write from me. Tell them your dog taught you.

> **Hint: All sentences have capitals and, remember, end marks—periods, question marks or, once a year, exclamation points.**

I recommend you now take a week off from writing and concentrate on reading and discussing ideas with your parents.

RECORD OF PROGRESS

Name:_____ Date:_____

Exercise # 1. **FOLLOWING DIRECTIONS**

This is the best sentence I wrote this week.

_____

_____

This mistake I made this week and I will not make it next week.

_____

_____

This is the sentence that had this mistake in it.

_____

_____

This is the sentence again showing how I fixed this mistake.

_____

_____

Comments:

#2 SENTENCE AND PARAGRAPH CONTROL

SKILL: BASIC

It may take you nine days to learn how to:
1. Include more than one piece of information in a sentence
2. Understand the relationship between main and supporting ideas
3. Write a paragraph so that it will include all the information you want it to and do so in an organized way

PREWRITING

Days One and Two:

Remember when you were little and you read books for small children? They sounded something like this:

> *Billy lived in a large house. The house was painted white. Billy lived with his mother, his father and his dog. Billy called his dog Fred.*

This is called Dick and Jane writing. It's fine for little kids, but you're good enough at reading now so that you shouldn't need to read books like that or to write that way. This exercise will teach you how to combine your ideas so your writing won't sound like a Dick and Jane book.

You're to **add five pieces** of information to a **core sentence**. You'll **write the sentence five times,** each time **adding one new piece** of information to the core sentence and what you have already added to it. **Do you need to read this again?** You might ask your parent what a core sentence is.

Each sentence will then be longer than the one before it. **You'll not always be able to add the new information to the end of the sentence.** You may have to **rewrite the whole sentence.** (Notice when I do this in the example on the next page.)

On the next page is an example of how you're to add information to a core sentence:

Core Sentence: *The frog ate the fly.* To this example I added the answers to the following questions:

1) What **time** was it?
2) What **season** was it?
3) **Who saw** the frog do it?
4) What did the **frog think** while she was eating the fly?
5) What was the **frog sitting on?**

Note: Below are the **five sentences** I wrote adding the above information **one item each time.** This example is written in **past tense.** (Past tense is when things have already happened. *John saw Bob.* <u>Not</u> *John sees Bob.*)

Notice that I **didn't always put** the new information at the **end of the sentences** and that each sentence **contains all the information** given in the sentences before it.

1) *It was **nine o'clock in the morning** when the frog ate the fly.*

2) *It was nine o'clock that **spring** morning when the frog ate the fly.*

3) *A raccoon saw the frog eat the fly at nine o'clock that morning last spring.*

4) *The frog **thought it was yummy** to eat the fly at nine o'clock in the morning last spring, but she didn't know the raccoon saw her do it.*

5) *The **frog was sitting on a lily pad** at nine o'clock that morning last spring when she thought it was yummy to eat the fly the raccoon saw her eat.*

Below is a chart showing how the answers to questions will give the information that is to be added to the core sentence.

HOW THE QUESTIONS PRODUCE INFORMATION

QUESTION	ANSWER
1. What **time** was it. . . ?	1. It was **nine o'clock**
2. What **season** was it. . . ?	2. Nine o'clock that **spring.**
3. **Who saw** the frog. . . ?	3. **Racoon** saw the frog
4. What did the **frog think**. . . ?	4. The frog **thought it was yummy**
5. What was the **frog sitting on.** ?	5. Sitting on a **lily pad** that morning

---

Hint: Remember capitals and end marks.

7

WRITING

You're to **add five pieces of information**, to the **core sentence** below. You'll get **these pieces of information** from **answering the questions** listed below. Show your paper to your parent at the start of day three.

Notice: the example core sentence is in **past tense**: *The frog ate the fly*. **Present tense** would be: *The frog eats the fly*.

Core sentence: *The boy found the dog*.

1. How **old** was the **boy**?
2. What **color** was the **dog**?
3. What **kind of dog** did the boy find?
4. What did the boy use to **tie the dog**?
5. **Where was the boy** when he found the dog?

Write your answers to these questions on another sheet of paper. You will then leave a clean book for someone else to use. Set your paper up like this example page if that will help you:

Answer to question 1. (*old was the boy?*) _____

_____

2. (*color of dog?*) _____

_____

3. (*kind of dog?*) _____

_____

4. (*used to tie up the dog?*) _____

_____

5. (*where was the boy?*) _____

Days Three and Four:
Your paper is to be given to your parent at the start of day five. You're to do to a new core sentence (*next page*) what I did to the core sentence in the example.

You're to write the idea of the following core sentence **five times**, adding **new information each time**. The new ideas will come from the answers to the questions below. **Do this on other paper**, but set your paper up like the following example.

Note: The core sentence is in **present tense**. This means that each of your sentences will have to be in present tense. (*Present tense means that you must write as if the events are happening as you write about them*)

Core Sentence - *The girl flies the kite.* (*See? The girl is flying the kite as you read.*)

1. **Who sees** the girl fly the kite?
2. What is the **girl's name**?
3. What **color is the kite**?
4. What is the **age** of the girl?
5. What is the **weather** like?

Sentence 1. (*who sees the girl?*) _____

_____

2. (*girl's name?*) _____

_____

3 (*color of the kite?*) _____

_____

4. (*age of the girl?*) _____

_____

5. (*what's the weather?*) _____

_____

> **Hint: Check your tenses.**

9

Days Five and Six:

On other paper, write your own core sentence and list of five questions.

Your core sentence _____

Your question 1. _____

_____

2. _____

_____

3. _____

_____

4. _____

_____

5. _____

On other paper, add the information to the core sentence by answering the five questions. Add one new piece of information each time you rewrite the sentence. This is to be finished and given to your parent at the start of day seven.

The five answers to your five questions:

1. _____   4. _____

2. _____   5. _____

3. _____

Write five new sentences with the information you get with the five answers:

Sentence 1. _____

_____

Sentence 2. _____

_____

Sentence 3. _____

_____

Sentence 4. _____

_____

Sentence 5. _____

_____

Day Seven:

Writing a paragraph is similar to writing a sentence. It has three steps:

Step #1. You must decide the on **subject** of you paragraph and **what information you** want your paragraph to give.

Step #2. You must **make a list** of this information. (This can be a list of words. It doesn't have to be a list of full sentences.)

Step #3. There must be a **topic sentence**. This is a sentence which tells the reader the main idea of the paragraph. The topic sentence will come first.

Example:

Step #1. If I were doing this exercise, I might want to write a paragraph about an old stuffed toy that had been in a closet for years.

Step #2. I would list the things about the stuffed bear I would put in the paragraph:

1). The kind of animal it was   *5). The number of limbs missing*
2). The material used to make it   *6). The holes and worn spots*
3). The condition of its fur   *7). The stuffing that was missing*
4). The condition of its ears and eyes   *8). How dirty it was*

> **Hint: Avoid subject verb patterns in your sentences.**
> **(Jane saw, I ran, Mom said, We went)**

11

Each of these **eight points** would have to be **turned into a sentence**. I'd have to decide what information **each sentence** would contain.

Below is an example for the first point, #1. *"The kind of animal it was"*
A) *Looked like a **fat bear***
B) ***Baby** bear*
C) ***Happy**, it was smiling*
D) *It was **holding out its arms***

Example of first sentence: (Note the underlining which shows where the information came from in the above list.)

> *I recognized my wonderful old <u>bear</u> when I first saw its <u>happy</u>, <u>fat</u>, <u>baby face</u> <u>smiling</u> at me as it <u>held out its arms</u> to be picked up.*

Step#3. Once the eight sentences were written, I would need to write a topic sentence. A topic sentences introduces the reader to the **information** that will be in a paragraph.

Example topic sentence (This would give my reader the main idea of my paragraph.):

> *I had been told to clean my room and was feeling very low until I opened my closet and noticed, in a far, dark corner, an old and very dear friend from years ago.*

On other paper, write for day eight:

Point #1. (the *idea* of your paragraph)

_____

Point #2. The list of descriptive points, not sentences, for your paragraph.

1) _____

2) _____

3) _____

4) _____

5) _____

> Hint: The structure of your sentences should vary.

Write your first sentence made from this listing. **Do this and all writing on other paper.** But, wait. Read on before you start to write that first sentence. You'll have to decide what tense you're going to use. It will be easiest for you to use past tense. This means that you will have to talk about things as if they had already happened.

Tense._____

You must decide what person to use. My **example is** written in **first person**. Notice the use of the word, *I.*

You can write in **first** person or in **third** person.

First person looks like this: *I saw the bear.*
Third person looks like this: *He saw the bear.*

Make a note of the person you will use.

Person: _____

Write the first sentence for the body of your paragraph on other paper. Set it up like the lines below. (from number 1, from the point #2 on page 12)

This first sentence you are to write will **not be the topic sentence** of your paragraph. It will be the **first sentence after** the **topic sentence**. You haven't written the topic sentence yet. On other paper, write:

1) (First sentence of the body) _____

_____

Days Eight and Nine:
    On the other paper write the rest of the sentences for the body of your paragraph.

2) _____

_____

3) _____

_____

4) _____

_____

5) _____

_____

Point#3. When you're ready to write the topic sentence, let your parent see your work.

Your topic sentence will tell your reader what information you'll give in the body of your paragraph. **Do this on other paper.**

Topic sentence: _____

_____

_____

Rewrite the paragraph putting the topic sentence first so that all of your paragraph will be on one page and in the right order (*topic sentence first*). Remember to indent the first line of your paragraph. Ask if you're not sure how to do this.

You're to turn in the finished paper at the start of day ten. Set up your paper to be like this example.

(Your Name)

(Skip two spaces)
                   (Your Title - It could be: *My Paragraph.*)
(Skip a line)
        (The first line of your paragraph (the topic sentence). Remember to indent it. Write the body of your paragraph. Skip *no* lines..)

(Have the same margins on all edges of the page.)

| **Hint: Go back and check your tense and person choices.** |

I recommend you now take a week off from writing and concentrate on reading and discussing ideas with your parents.

RECORD OF PROGRESS

Name:_____ Date:_____

Exercise #2 **SENTENCE AND PARAGRAPH CONTROL**

This is the best sentence I wrote this week.

_____

_____

This mistake I made this week and I will not make it next week.

_____

_____

This is the sentence that had this mistake in it.

_____

_____

This is the sentence again showing how I fixed this mistake.

_____

_____

Comments:

#3 WRITE AND REWRITE A SENTENCE

SKILL: BASIC

It may take you four days to learn to:
1. Write a simple sentence
2. Make a simple sentence more complicated
3. Connect a number of sentences to make a story

PREWRITING

Day One:

We all know that a sentence has a person, place or a thing in it doing something. A sentence sounds like this: *The bug looked at a spider.* The bug is a thing doing something. What the bug is doing is looking at a spider.

This exercise will help you write longer and better sentences. I'll do the first exercise to show you how easy this is. *The bug looked at a spider.*

I rewrote this sentence and left a blank for a word that would describe the spider.

1. *The bug looked at a _____ spider.*

I had to think of a number of words that could go into that blank space. Words that would describe the spider. Here are ten I thought I might be able to use:

1) hairy   2) gray   3) hungry   4) wicked   5) pretty
6) big   7) scary   8) small   9) girl   10) ugly

I picked number 3. which gave me: *The bug looked at a **hungry** spider.*

2. Now that I'd written the sentence with the word I chose in it, I had to rewrite the sentence again telling what the **bug** was like.

Getting ready to do that, the sentence looked like this: *The_____ **bug** looked at a **hungry** spider.*

> **Hint: Remember what makes up a full sentence?**

16

Then I had to think of ten words that would describe the bug:

1) small   2) hungry   3) frightened   4) fuzzy   5) mad
6) green   7) quick   8) sick   9) large   10) spider-eating

Using one of these choices (#10) in my sentence, I came up with: *The spider-eating bug looked at a hungry spider*.

Poor little guys.

WRITING

You're to write, **on other paper,** a short sentence like the one I wrote at the start of this exercise: *"The bug looked at a spider."* Try not to write about a bug and a spider.

_____

_____

_____

Make a listing like this one of ten words that you could use in that sentence to describe the person, place or thing. **Do this on other paper.**

1) _____   6) _____

2) _____   7) _____

3) _____   8) _____

4) _____   9) _____

5) _____   10) _____

Pick one of these ten words and write, on other paper, the sentence again using that word in it.

_____

_____

17

Make another list of ten words that describe another part of your sentence.

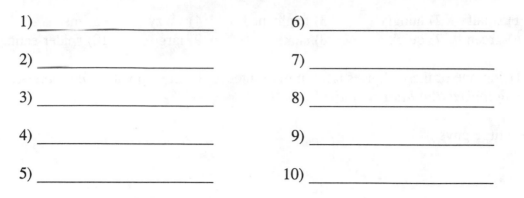

1) _____   6) _____

2) _____   7) _____

3) _____   8) _____

4) _____   9) _____

5) _____   10) _____

Pick one of these ten words and write the sentence again using this new word in it.

_____

_____

Days Two Through Four:

Using other paper, write a very short story for very young children about a kitten that is being raised by a mother duck. The kitten will think it is a baby duck. It will do duck-like things. You'll describe what a kitten who thinks it's a duck might do.

There should be at **least four sentences** about **each** of the following ideas:

1. What did the kitten do when the rest of the **ducklings ate corn**?
2. What did the kitten do when the rest of the **ducklings went into the pond**?
3. What did the kitten do when the rest of the **ducklings followed their mother**?
4. What did the rest of the ducklings do when the **kitten chased a mouse**?

When you're writing this very short story, **add information** to your **sentences** just like you did on the early part of this exercise. Set your paper up like this example.

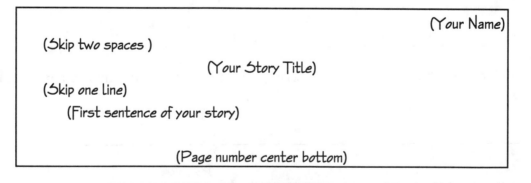

Hint: Remember sentence structure variety and tense and person consistency.

I recommend you now take a week off from writing and concentrate on reading and discussing ideas with your parents.

RECORD OF PROGRESS

Name:_____ Date:_____

Exercise #3 **WRITE AND REWRITE A SENTENCE**

This is the best sentence I wrote this week.

_____

_____

This mistake I made this week and I will not make it next week.

_____

_____

This is the sentence that had this mistake in it.

_____

_____

This is the sentence again showing how I fixed this mistake.

_____

_____

Comments:

#4 DESCRIPTION OF MY FRIEND

SKILL: DESCRIPTION

It may take you four days to learn to:
1. Organize what you will describe
2. Describe in sentences what a friend looks like
3. Have your parent read your paper with you
4. Rewrite the parts you and your parent feel can be improved

PREWRITING

Day One:

This exercise will give you a chance to write about one of your friends. The first thing you'll have to do is make a list of the characteristics your friend has. (what he/she looks and acts like) This list should include:

1. Height
2. Weight
3. Color
   A. Skin
   B. Hair
   C. Eyes
4. Speech
   A. Pitch of voice
   B. Favorite expressions
   C. Loudness

5. Activities
   A. Hobbies
   B. School work
   C. Sports
   D. TV programs
6. The things you like best
   about this person

Make yourself a form like the one below if it will help you.

1. **Height:**_____ 2. **Weight:** _____ 3. **Color** of skin:_____ Hair: ____ Eyes:____

4. **Speech:** A. Pitch:_____ B. Expressions: 1) _____

2.) _____ 3) _____

C. Loudness: _____

5. **Activities:** A: Hobbies: _____

    B. School work: _____ C. TV programs:_____

    _____

6. The **things I like** about this person: _____

    _____

WRITING

Days Two and Three:

Once you have a list of characteristics you can write about, you'll have to introduce your friend to your reader. We'll call this part of your paper the **introduction**.

This **introduction** should include your friend's:
1. Name
2. Grade
3. Address (This should be both town and state.)

This introduction might read like this: (The three points in the above list are numbered in this example only to show you where the three pieces of information came from.)

   (1.) _Janet Brown_ is one of my best friends in the (2) _tenth grade_. Janet lives near my house on (3) _Elm Street in St. Louis._

Set up your introduction on other paper to be like this sample:

INTRODUCTION (Your introduction will not have a title.)

_____

_____

_____

_____

_____

_____

Hint: Remember Dick and Jane writing? Check for it.

In the body of your paper you'll tell about your friend. There should be at least two sentences for each of the items on the list you just wrote. If your list is like my suggested list, you should have **at least** two sentences about your friend's **height**. Then there should be **at least** two sentences about your friend's **weight,** then at least two or more about **color**.

You might want to review exercise #2 where you learned to write with detail.

You should **use as much detail** in your description as you can. It would be good if you were to **use examples**. When you tell about your friend's eyes, you should do more than say just that they're blue or brown. Tell how your friend **uses** her eyes. This might read like this:

When Janet is thinking, her brown eyes get big and round, and then she half closes them. When this happens, I know she is thinking of something that she likes very much.

When you tell about your friend's hair, you should say more than that it's brown. You should give details about how it's cut and what your friend does with it:

John's hair is longer than his mother would like it to be, but John likes it long. He is always pushing it out of his face with his fingers. He has a lot of trouble with it when we play ball.

When you write about what your friend's speech is like, it might be good to use examples to show your reader how your friend talks. It can read like this:

Bill is a little shy. When someone asks him a question, he answers in a very low voice. Even when he knows the answer, sometimes he doesn't say it. But when we're playing ball, it changes. Then it is as loud as mine.

It would be good if you write only nice things about your friend. Your paper may be read by other people and you wouldn't want to hurt your friend's feelings. When you write your paper, be sure to include the things that are shown on the following list and the **outline** on the next page.

1. Put your name in the top right corner of the page.
2. Put a title on the first line. It might be: *My Friend*. (Notice the capital letters and that there are no quotation marks. This is because it is your title.)
3. Skip the first line after the title
4. Write your introduction (Do not skip any other lines.)
5. Write the description of your friend using the lists you have created.

> **Hint: Remember to put detail in your sentences.**

When you feel that your paper is finished, check each part of it against the listing on page 20 to make sure you have included all the parts in your finished paper and that they are in the right place.

Day Four:

Parts of your paper probably have been proofread by you and your parent many times. Write the final copy and check it again.

I recommend you now take a week off from writing and concentrate on reading and discussing ideas with your parents.

RECORD OF PROGRESS

Assignment # 4 **DESCRIPTION OF MY FRIEND**

This is the best sentence I wrote this week.

_____

_____

This mistake I made this week and I will not make it next week.

_____

_____

This is the sentence that had this mistake in it.

_____

_____

This is the sentence again showing how I fixed this mistake.

_____

_____

Comments:

#5 POINT OF VIEW

SKILL: CREATION

It may take you four days to learn that:
1. Characters in stories can be shown to think as they talk
2. You can create characters who think

PREWRITING

Days One and Two:

When you write fiction, it can be fun to tell your readers **what the people in your stories are thinking.** This means that instead of telling your readers just what happens, you can **tell how the characters feel and what they want**.

I'll write a short piece both ways:
The first way: **Not telling** what the characters are thinking
The second way: **Telling** what the characters are thinking and feeling

Not telling what the characters are thinking

Bill liked to play practical jokes. It was his little brother's job to collect the pop bottles each week and count them and then figure out how much money they would bring at the bottle return counter.

This week Bill hid one bottle until after his brother had counted them and figured out how much money they would bring, then he put that bottle in the sack. Of course, when his mother turned in the bottles, there were more than Bill's brother had counted. There were too many bottles and too much money.

Next week Bill hid two bottles and put them in the sack when his mother was ready to return them. Again Bill's little brother was surprised to be short by two bottles. Bill's mother asked Bill if he would help his brother figure out the number of bottles the next week.

On the third week Bill put three bottles aside. Again Bill's mother had Bill's brother count the bottles and figure out the money. After Bill had put the three hidden bottles in the sack, Bill's mother said to Bill, "Bill, you've been kind to help your little brother figure out the bottle return money. If he's correct this week, I'll give you ten times as much as the return of the bottles brings."

In this short piece, the reader doesn't know what any of the people in the story are thinking. The reader could guess that Bill thinks he's having a good time fooling his brother, but not be sure. The reader doesn't know if Bill's mother guesses what Bill's doing and "turns the tables" on him. Next I'll write this piece and put in what the characters are thinking. I think you'll see that it makes better reading.

Telling what the characters are thinking and feeling

Bill liked to play practical jokes. It was his little brother's job to collect the pop bottles each week and count them and then figure out how much money they would bring at the bottle return counter at the store.

One week Bill hid one bottle until after his brother had counted the bottles and figured out how much money they would bring. He then put that bottle in the sack with the others. **He laughed when he thought** *of his mother discovering that his brother hadn't counted right.*

Of course, when their mother turned in the bottles, there were more than Bill's brother had counted. There were too many bottles; there was too much money. **This surprised Bill's mother, and she thought,** *"My young son is good at counting and figuring out the money. Something must be going on."*

The next week Bill hid two bottles and put them in the sack when his mother was ready to return them. Again Bill's little **brother was surprised** *to be short by two bottles. Bill's mother watched Bill's face when she explained that the count had been off by two bottles. She saw Bill smiling at the news.*

Bill's mother thought, *"It might be a good idea to teach Bill something about dealing honestly with others." Bill's mother asked Bill, "Next week will you help your brother figure out the number of bottles?"*

On the third week, Bill put three bottles aside. After Bill had put the three hidden bottles in the sack, Bill's mother said, as she was carrying the sack out the door, "Bill, you have been kind to help your little brother figure out the bottle return money. If he's correct this week, I'll give you ten times as much as the return of the bottles brings."

WRITING

You'll write a short piece about some person who plays practical jokes and then gets caught by others. Don't tell your reader what the characters are thinking. If you can't think of a practical joke, that's fine, just tell about something that a person does that's not a good thing to do and the person gets caught at it. It doesn't have to be a joke.

Days Three and Four:
Write the same short story, but this time tell the reader what the joker and the other characters are thinking.

Hint: Commas go inside quote marks.

Look below at the examples to find out how to punctuate characters' thoughts. Each time you want your reader to know what a character is thinking, you'll have to start your sentence in **one of the three ways** shown in the examples below:

1. *He thought, "This week I'll put one extra bottle in the sack."*

2. *He thought about adding two extra bottles the next week.* (Note: no quote marks)

3. If you want to, you can give a character's thoughts in the first part of the sentence and then tell the reader that this is what the character <u>is</u> thinking. It looks like this:

   "I'll put four bottles in the sack the next time," Bill thought.

Notice (underlined in #3 above), that when I talk about what's going on in a story, I always use present tense.

Present tense looks like this: *The boy in that story **feeds** his snakes.* Use of present tense in talking about a story that has been written in past tense may not make sense, but it has to be done this way.

This doesn't always sound right, but you'll get used to it and it's the right way to talk about literature, painting and sculpture. More about this later.

> **Hint: Quotations start with capitals.**

I recommend you now take a week off from writing and concentrate on reading and discussing ideas with your parents.

RECORD OF PROGRESS

Name:_____ Date:_____

Exercise **#5 POINT OF VIEW**

This is the best sentence I wrote this week.

_____

_____

This mistake I made this week and I will not make it next week.

_____

_____

This is the sentence that had this mistake in it.

_____

_____

This is the sentence again showing how I fixed this mistake.

_____

_____

Comments:

#6 "WHAT DID YOU DO TODAY?"

SKILL: ORGANIZATION

It may take you four days to learn:
1. How to organize a description
2. How to use your own experience to help you to learn to organize
3. How to plan an organized answer to the question all parents ask: "What did you do today?"

PREWRITING

Day One:

Because your parents love you, they ask you what you do in your schooling. They want to share your day with you.

If you were to say, "Nothing," they'd be disappointed. If you kept saying, "Nothing," when they asked, they'd stop asking. You wouldn't want that to happen.

They don't want to know everything you did; they want to know just the exciting things you learned and what you did that you liked.

This is where organizing will help you. Create pages like the ones below.

Step 1. List on other paper, for a recent day's schooling, the things you did that you liked.

1. _____

2. _____

3. _____

4. _____

5. _____

Step 2. You had periods when you studied, ate, listened to lectures, read, played games, watched movies or were just bored. List those periods on another page like the one below:

1. _____

2. _____

3. _____

4. _____

5. _____

6. _____

WRITING

Days Two through Four:

1. You should describe one or two things you did in each of the periods you think your parents might find interesting. Set your paper up like this example:

(Your Name)

What I Found Interesting

Period 1.   The first thing I did today was to work with Bill on our science project. We're making a volcano that erupts. We've been trying to figure out how to make the sides of the mountain without the plaster all running down. We had a hard time of it, but we decided to make the sides of the volcano out of chicken wire. Tomorrow we're going to see if we can get the plaster to stick to the wire.
Period 2.   I worked on the bow. I used the template that dad showed me how to make and I spent about an hour trimming around the hand grip. I had to be careful not to trim too much.
Period 3.   The best thing that happened was when I got my report back. I got a B+ on it. It would have been an A if it'd been typed.

Page number bottom center

Hint: An apostrophe shows possession. (Bill's idea)

2. After you've written something for each period, your next step is to pick out one or two of the things you did that were the most exciting.

You should write in detail about one or two things and set this paper to be like the following example:

(Your Name)

The Most Exciting Thing That Happened

Bill and I had a real talk about how the volcano should look. I think that it should have some of the rim broken away, like it's been blown off in the past. Bill wants it to be perfectly round, like it's a new one. I even got pictures from the library to show him that most of them aren't perfectly round, but you know Bill.

Page number bottom center

---

3. Have your parent check your writing to make sure there are no serious problems with it.

Keep this paper handy to review just before you're asked, "What did you do today?"

> **Hint: Use an apostrophe for contractions. Put it where the letter(s) is/are missing. (It is, It's)**

I recommend you now take a week off from writing and concentrate on reading and discussing ideas with your parents.

RECORD OF PROGRESS

Name:_____ Date:_____

Exercise #6 "WHAT DID YOU DO TODAY?"

This is the best sentence I wrote this week.

_____

_____

This mistake I made this week and I will not make it next week.

_____

_____

This is the sentence that had this mistake in it.

_____

_____

This is the sentence again showing how I fixed this mistake.

_____

_____

Comments:

PROBLEMS I HAVE SOLVED THIS FIRST SEMESTER

1. _____

_____

2. _____

_____

3. _____

_____

4. _____

_____

5. _____

_____

6. _____

_____

7. _____

_____

8. _____

_____

How I feel about this progress I'm making:

_____

_____

FIRST SEMESTER REPORT
on
WRITING SKILLS MASTERY

THIRD LEVEL WRITING EXERCISES

Student Name:_____ Date:_____

Skill   Needs
Mastered   Experience

Exercise 1: Following Directions
Skill Area: Basic

____	____	1. Believing that it is possible to follow directions
____	____	2. Understanding that it is good to follow directions
____	____	3. Understanding what makes a sentence

Exercise 2: Sentence and Paragraph Control
Skill Area: Basic

____	____	1. Including more than one item in a sentence
____	____	2. Understanding the relationship between main and subordinate ideas
____	____	3. Writing an organized paragraph

Exercise 3: Write and Rewrite a Sentence
Skill Area: Basic

____	____	1. Writing a simple sentence
____	____	2. Making a simple sentence more complicated
____	____	3. Connecting a number of complicated sentences to make a story

Skill   Needs
Mastered Experience

Exercise 4: My Friend
Skill Area: Description

Skill Mastered	Needs Experience	
____	____	1. Organizing what will be described
____	____	2. Describing in sentences the appearance of a friend
____	____	3. Seeking help from a teacher
____	____	4. Rewriting parts of a paper to improve it

Exercise 5: Point of View
Skill Area: Creation

Skill Mastered	Needs Experience	
____	____	1. Understanding that characters think when they talk
____	____	2. Writing about characters who think

Exercise 6: "What Did You Do Today?"
Skill Area: Organization

Skill Mastered	Needs Experience	
____	____	1. Organizing a description
____	____	2. Using experiences to help organize
____	____	3. Planning organized answers to questions

#7 FURNITURE

SKILL: ORGANIZATION

It may take you five days to:
1. Examine the placement of a number of objects
2. Organize a description of objects so that their placement and characteristics can be understood

PREWRITING

Day One:

You must organize a description of the furniture in the living room of your house or apartment. You should include in this paper:
1. The **number** of pieces of furniture
2. The **kinds** of pieces
3. The **colors**
4. The **placement**
5. The **materials** the pieces are **made of** or the type of material that is used for a **covering**

All of these pieces must be organized so that when your parent reads your paper, your parent will be able to tell you:
1. **Where the pieces are** in the room
2. What they **look like**
3. What they're **used for**

These three things will be what your parent will look for in your final paper, so this will be like a test on how well you've organized all of this material. Check for these three things before you hand in your paper.

Some of the work on this paper will have to be done in a place away from your usual desk. We'll call it *homework*. Your first job is to takes notes on each of the items on your list. Start with number 1: *The number of pieces*. You will have to have this handy when you start day two. (Put it in your shoe so you don't forget it.)

Day Two:

Check with a parent to see if you've forgotten anything like rugs or pictures. It might help if you make a map of your living room so that you can remember where everything is. Writing about placement isn't hard to do, but if you haven't done it before it could get confusing. But then, if you knew everything you'd be a genius.

Make a list like this of the **number of pieces of each type of furnishing**: (If this listing is not like your house, change it.)

1. Rugs or floor covering: _____   2. Pictures: _____   3. Chairs: _____

4. Couches: _____   5. footstools: _____   6. Other kinds of decorations: _____

7. Tables: _____

WRITING

Day Three:

Start writing your paper. For this exercise you **don't have to write in sentences** or in paragraphs. This exercise can be done in **lists**. A list can be made of **words, phrases, sentences or paragraphs**. Use whatever seems best to show the organization of the furniture. Your paper might even look like this example:

```
                                                      (Your Name)



                        Number of Pieces


     1. East wall—One couch, one lamp, two pictures, one pizza box


     2. North wall—Two chairs on the east end of the wall—one on the
        west end of the wall


     3. West wall—One small table and one lamp


     4. South wall—One arch into the kitchen and the stairs to the
        second floor.
                     Page number bottom center
```

> **Hint: Unless they're full sentences, items in lists don't always need periods, but they do start with capitals.**

Your description of the placement of the pieces could read like the this example.

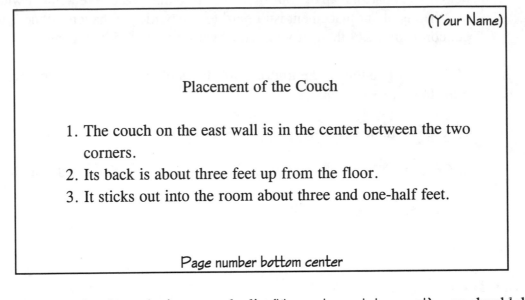

When you write about the items on the list (like number and placement), you should do all of **them in the same order**. For example, notice in the sample I wrote for you that I started with the east wall and then went to the west wall. If you start the first item on the east wall, you should do all of the rest of the items the same way. You then should start with the east wall when you talk about sizes, and start with the east wall when you talk about colors, and so on.

Make sure your parent sees your work today.

Days Four and Five:
You should be able to finish your lists by the end of day five. If you're not done, that's not bad. Your parent may let you take another day on this problem or suggest that you finish it for day six.

> **Hint: Sentences in lists do need periods.**

I recommend you now take a week off from writing and concentrate on reading and discussing ideas with your parents.

RECORD OF PROGRESS

Name:_____ Date:_____

Exercise **#7 FURNITURE**

This is the best sentence I wrote this week.

_____

_____

This mistake I made this week and I will not make it next week.

_____

_____

This is the sentence that had this mistake in it.

_____

_____

This is the sentence again showing how I fixed this mistake.

_____

_____

Comments:

#8 OUT THE WINDOW

SKILL: DESCRIPTION

It may take you three days to learn that:
1. All people do not see the same things
2. There is a way to tell where someone was by knowing what that person could see
3. What you see can be organized

PREWRITING

Day One:

We all see things differently. This is because we're all in different places. Sometimes the differences are not too great, but there will always be small differences because of the angles from which we're looking. Your parent may want to talk about this idea with you and then give you a demonstration of how this works.

You'll describe what you can see out the window of a room in your house.

WRITING

When you **describe** things, you should **start with general statements** and then write about the **details.** Your paper might start like this example of a first sentence:

Looking out the window from my desk, I can see the back of our neighbor's house and the fence at the back of our lot.

A list of the areas or groups of things you can see might look like this:

1. *There is a swing on one side of the back yard.*
2. *There is one of the goal posts on the soccer field for the school.*
3. *Two dogs are chasing each other, and our neighbor is picking up pieces of the tree that came down in the storm last night.*

> **Hint: A compound sentence needs a comma before the conjunction, and you should put one there.**

On other paper list the groups of things you can see. (*There can be any number*):

1_____ 2_____

3_____ 4_____

Days Two and Three:

You'll want to describe in detail the things you've just listed. You should start with the first one. For the first thing you can see, your paper might look like this:

(Your Name)

The First Thing I Can See

The sand in front of the dog's house is still wet looking and has leaves in it that were blown there in the storm last night. I can see the edge of the dog's house and even see where his chain has worn all the grass away in a circle around the front of his house.

Write on other paper the list of the groups of things you can see. (If you want to use 2 or 4 groups, that's fine.)

Day Four:

Using your lists, write your paper as *one* paper about what you can see from your window. There should be **a number of sentences** about each of the things you can see for each paragraph in your paper. Set your final paper up to look like this example:

(Your Name)

(Skip two spaces)

Your Title

(Skip a Line)

(Your Description)
Looking out the window from my desk, I can see the back of our neighbor's house and the fence at the back of our lot.

Page number bottom center

I recommend you now take a week off from writing and concentrate on reading and discussing ideas with your parents.

41

RECORD OF PROGRESS

Name:_____ Date:_____

Exercise #8 OUT THE WINDOW

This is the best sentence I wrote this week.

_____

_____

This mistake I made this week and I will not make it next week.

_____

_____

This is the sentence that had this mistake in it.

_____

_____

This is the sentence again showing how I fixed this mistake.

_____

_____

Comments:

#9 A VERY SHORT STORY

SKILL: CREATION

It may take you five days to:
1. Plan a very short children's story
2. Write the parts of a very short children's story
3. Put these parts together

PREWRITING

Day One:

All stories have the same parts. The very short stories in books for small children have the same parts that the long stories have that you and your parents read. All stories have:

1. **Characters**   3. **Ways the characters solve the problems**
2. **Problems**   4. **Endings**

You'll be able to write a good, very short story for small children if you include these four parts. To show you how easy this is, I've written one, and, if you follow the above outline, you'll be able to write a story that you'll be proud of.

1. **Character:**   A frog named Hortense. She's a beautiful, young girl frog.

2. **Problem:**   Hortense has a problem. Her tongue has lost its sticky so she can't catch anything to eat.

3. **Solving the Problem**   Hortense has help from Freddy, an ugly boy frog. He shows her how to dip her tongue in flowers to get pollen on it to make it sticky again.

4. **An ending:**   Now Hortense can catch flies like all the other frogs. She's so happy that she marries Freddy and they teach their children how to make their tongues stay sticky.

> **Hint: All punctuation marks go inside quotation marks.**

The next step was to put the characters in a place: I first tried the library, then I decided that a pond might be a better place for frogs.

The main characters must have personality. (*Look at the example below*):

1. **Hortense** is a very beautiful frog. She loses the sticky on her tongue when she spends so much time cleaning her slick body to keep herself beautiful.
2. **Freddy** is ugly but very smart. He loves Hortense.

Now I was ready to write the story. I numbered the above list of four story parts so you could spot them quickly in this story. Notice that there are two main characters. They both have problems, but different ones. Both problems are solved.

Hortense and Freddy
a
Sticky Romance

1. (Character #1) Hortense knew she was beautiful. In fact, she was so pleased at how good looking she was, she spent most of her days gazing at her reflection in the surface of the pond where she lived. If there was even a speck of dirt on her slick, green body, she would flick it off with her long and sticky tongue.

2. (Character #1 Problem) One day, after cleaning herself until she almost sparkled in the morning sun, she found her tongue was no longer sticky. She had worn all the sticky off. When she tried to catch food, the bugs bounced off her tongue. Dragonflies perched on her head, and spiders sat in the shade she made on her lily pad and ignored her.

Surrounded by food, Hortense was starving. She grew thin and began to lose her beauty.

Now, when she slowly flicked her tongue against her dull skin, the dirt would smear, and she spent much of her time silently weeping. Hortense feared she would die if she couldn't catch flies, and she couldn't if she had no sticky on her tongue. She sat on her lily pad and cried, "Oh, what a beautiful but sad thing I am. I will starve and be lost to the world."

1. (Character #2) Freddy heard her sighing this way. He was large and very ugly, but he loved Hortense more than anything in his world. He swam to Hortense's lily pad and gazed at his beautiful dreamfrog.

Hortense had pressed the back of her thin and very pale hand against her brow. She jerked her hand down when she saw Freddy and said, in an angry but very weak voice,

2. (Character #2 Problem) "Go away, Freddy. You know I am too beautiful to pay any attention to you."

Freddy tried to smile through the pain he felt for Hortense and whispered up at her, "I heard you crying. Is there anything I can do to help?"

Hint: Your paragraphs need to be indented.

Hortense took a long breath and said, "No. I will just have to starve because I have lost the sticky on my tongue."

Freddy was smart, but this was a very serious problem. Thinking as hard as he ever had, he drifted to the bottom of the pond. Freddy stayed in the mud at the bottom for a long time. He rose to the surface only after he had thought of a way to save his beautiful Hortense.

On the bank near their pond, Freddy found a small field of flowers. When he stuck his tongue into the center of a blossom, the pollen made it so sticky that catching a fly was one of the easiest things he'd ever done.

Freddy swam quickly out to his lovely Hortense. Holding onto the edge of her lily pad and gazing up into her sad face, he said, "Hortense, I love you. If I tell you how to get your tongue sticky again, will you be my girlfrog?" Hortense was still for so long Freddy began to think she had not heard him. Hortense turned slowly and looked down at Freddy over her narrow and thinning nose.

3. (Characters #1 & #2 Solutions to problems) It was after many agreements were reached that Freddy and Hortense swam toward the bank and the field of blue blossoms.

4. (Ending) Today, if you were to go to that same pond, you might see beautiful small frogs who slide the tips of their tongues into the center of flowers.

And, if you had time to wait and were very lucky, you might see larger, and not-so-pretty frogs who spend long periods of time lying in the mud at the bottom of the pond, thinking.

It's not necessary to write such a long short story. This story can be much shorter. I'll show you how it could be written as a very, very short story. Your story should **not** be this short. You'll see (because I've numbered them) that the four parts are still here.

Hortense

1. (Character #1) Hortense, a girl frog 2. (Character 2 problem) who was too beautiful for (1. Character #2) Freddy, 2. (Character 1 problem) lost the sticky on her tongue. Freddy, who loved her, thought of a way to make her tongue sticky again.

He told her that he would tell her how to do this if she would be his girlfrog. Hortense agreed.

3. (Characters #1 & 2 solutions) Freddy told Hortense to put her tongue into a flower and the pollen would make it sticky. Hortense did this, and she was so pleased that she married Freddy. 4. (Ending) If you go to that pond, you will see baby frogs who put their tongues into flowers. They'll tell you that their mother showed them how.

Here are some characters with problems you might use for your children's story:

-The groundhog who lost her calendar
-The turtle who went for a walk and forgot where he had left his shell

> **Hint: Remember sentence structure variety.**

-The robin who didn't want to go south in the fall
-The rabbit who didn't want to eat her vegetables
-The owl who didn't know her name
-The frog who thought she was a bird

Your story doesn't have to be about animals. Use people, cars, houses or even fish. The same outline will work no matter who the character is or what the problem is. On other paper, list the character, the problem and the solution.

WRITING

Day Two:

Think of your character in a place for your story because you're now ready to start writing. You'll write about the character and the problem. Remember to have the characters talk to each other. This will make them come alive for your reader. Look at my story to see how to punctuate dialogue. On other paper, list the character and the place.

Day Three:

You'll write about how your character solves the problem.

Days Four and Five:

You'll write the ending to your story and put all of this together for your final copy. You should spend some of day five checking punctuation and spelling. Your final copy, the one you hand to your parents, should be set up like this example.

```
                                                          (Your Name)
                                                           (The Date)


(Skip two spaces )
                              (The Title of Your Story)
(Skip one line)
                              (Your Story Starts Here)


(Remember, margins on all edges of each page)


                         Page number bottom center
```

Hint: In dialogue, each new speaker gets a new paragraph.

I recommend you now take a week off from writing and concentrate on reading and discussing ideas with your parents.

RECORD OF PROGRESS

Name:_____ Date:_____

Exercise *#9 A VERY SHORT STORY*

This is the best sentence I wrote this week.

_____

_____

This mistake I made this week and I will not make it next week.

_____

_____

This is the sentence that had this mistake in it.

_____

_____

This is the sentence again showing how I fixed this mistake.

_____

_____

Comments:

#10 MY ROOM

SKILL: DESCRIPTION

It may take you five days to learn that:
1. The world around you is organized
2. To describe something you must understand its organization
3. You can help your reader understand what you think is important by describing things in organized ways

PREWRITING

Day One:

All things in nature are organized. Think about a tree. It's made up of cells. Each one has a job. Some cells are bark, some leaves, some roots and some are parts of the trunk and branches. All of the cells in a tree are organized for special jobs or the tree couldn't live. If the leaf cells were under the ground, the tree couldn't get water. Leaves don't work that way.

If you were to describe a tree, you'd have to understand how the tree cells were organized. To describe man-made things, you have to understand how they're organized, too. The organization of a shirt or a car is obvious. They're easy.

Some things are not organized so well. In a way similar to the way you organized the objects in exercise number 7, "Furniture," you'll describe the objects in your bedroom at home. But, this time the organization will be different.

The first step in writing a description of a collection of things is to understand what parts are involved. **List on other paper** the objects in your room. I'll start you off:

1. Electrical Equipment   5. _____

2. Dirty clothes   6. _____

3. Decorations   7. _____

4._____   8. _____

You shouldn't limit yourself to just eight things. You can have as many as you wish.

A good rule to follow when you have to make a decision about writing like this is to think about your reader. The point of writing is to help your reader understand something. What will make the most sense for your reader to read first in the list? You should put that item first.

There are a number of ways to organize objects, some of which are by their:
1. **Importance**   (the most important first and the least important last)
2. **Size**   (the biggest first)
3. **Value**   (the most expensive first)
4. **Location**   (the closest to a fixed point first)
5. **Place**   (in the alphabet)
6. **Number**   (the largest number of objects first and the least last)

Using one of these ways, re-order your list of the objects in your room. This means that you should write the list again. (Identify your method of organizing your list at the top of your page like this example)

(Re-organized by _____)

(List of objects)
1. _____

2. _____

3. _____

4. _____

5. _____

6. _____

7. _____

8. _____

Day Two:
You are to write a **paragraph** of description about **each item** on your list. Each one should contain **at least three or four sentences.** This is easy. The first paragraph about an object could read like the example below. (Notice that I used the importance of the objects to organized them. Underlined.)

> **Hint: First letters in a list should be capitalized.**

The most important thing in my room is, of course, my bed. It's the bottom half of a set of bunk beds I used to share with my brother. After he got his own room, we had to split up the bunk beds. He got the top half, so my bed has holes in the top of each corner where the legs of his bed used to fit. We always had lots of fun when we slept in the same room, but I like having my own room and my own bed now.

WRITING

If you write this much for each item on your list, you'll have a very good description of your room. You should finish the first three items on your list on day two.

Day Three:
Describe items 4, 5 and 6.

Day Four:
Describe items 7, and 8. If you think you've run out of things to describe, think of wall paper, moldings, ceiling fixtures, sports equipment, old toys in the back of the closet, dust mice under the bed and broken pencils in the top drawer.

Day Five:
Put your descriptions together in one paper. Set up your final copy like this example.

(Your Name)
(The Date)

(Skip two spaces)
(The Title of Your Paper)
(Skip a Line)
    I have an interesting room where I spend a lot of my time. Since it's my bedroom and where I study, and can name it anything I want to. I call it "The Cave."
    The most important thing in my room is, of course, my bed.

Page number bottom center

Hint: Neat isn't bad.

I recommend you now take a week off from writing and concentrate on reading and discussing ideas with your parents.

RECORD OF PROGRESS

Name:_____ Date:_____

Exercise #10 MY ROOM

This is the best sentence I wrote this week.

_____

_____

This mistake I made this week and I will not make it next week.

_____

_____

This is the sentence that had this mistake in it.

_____

_____

This is the sentence again showing how I fixed this mistake.

_____

_____

Comments:

#11 HOW PEOPLE MOVE WHEN THEY TALK

SKILL: DESCRIPTION

It may take you three days to learn to:
1. Punctuate dialogue
2. Describe characters' actions
3. Have your characters move as they talk together

PREWRITING

Day One:

It'll make your writing more fun to read when you have your characters talk to each other if you have them move their bodies as they talk.

For this exercise you'll have to watch how the members of your family move when they talk. See if the adults move any differently than the kids do. You'll find most people move their eyes, hands, feet, and their shoulders when they talk.

Just as real people move when they talk together, your characters, when you have them talking, should have body movement descriptions right along with what they say. It can read like the example below.

To show you how this works, I'll put the descriptions inside parentheses ( ) and make the printing bold: (If you ask nicely, your parent may read this to you.)

> *John was getting mad. His voice rose* **(and he waved his hands in the air)** *as he shouted, "I get the catcher's mitt!"*
> *Bill,* **(looking John in the eyes)**, *said "I get it today, I asked the coach yesterday."*
> *"You did not. I was there and you didn't say nothin' about today."*
> *John* **(pointed his finger at Bill's chest and)** *said, "I got the mitt and I'm gonna keep it." **(He put it behind his back.)***
> *Bill,* **(reaching behind John and trying to grab the mitt)** *said, "Give it to me."*
> *John said,* **(as he lifted his lip)**, *"Try and take it."*

Hint: Separate what a person says from the rest of the sentence by commas.

To show you how important it can be to let your reader see your characters move, I wrote this short conversation again and **took out** the movements. You'll recognize that it's harder to "see" the characters when they don't have bodies to go with their voices.

> *John was getting mad. His voice rose as he shouted, "I get the catcher's mitt!"*
> *Bill said right back at him, "I asked the coach yesterday."*
> *"You did not. I was there and you didn't say nothin' about today. I got the mitt and I'm gonna keep it."*
> *Bill said, "Give it to me."*
> *John said, "Try and take it."*

You will:
1. Decide on the **two characters** for your dialogue
2. Decide on **what kinds of people** they'll be
3. Decide what they'll **talk about**

Number 1: On other paper, give your two characters **names**:

A._____ B._____

Number 2: Describe what they'll **talk about**:

_____

_____

_____

_____

Number 3: Describe the **kinds of people** they are:

Character A.   Age:____ Sex:_____   List three words that describe this person:

1_____ 2_____ 3_____

Character B.   Age:____ Sex:_____   List three words that describe this person:

1_____ 2_____ 3_____

| Hint: All quotations begin with a capital. |

53

Day Two:

You'll decide on the setting for your dialogue. You **may** want to describe:

1. The **place**
2. The **time** of day

3. The **weather**
4. The **activity** at the time of the conversation

Number 1. The **Place:** _____

Number 2. The **Time:** _____

Number 3. The **Weather:** _____

Number 4. The **Activity** at the time of the conversation: _____

_____

WRITING

Days Three & Four:

Today and the next one you'll write the conversation. Knowing the above information is important for you, but it **won't be necessary** for you to **include all** of it in your dialogue.

I think it would be good for you to look at dialogue to see how to punctuate yours. Check on page 52.

> **Hint: All punctuation marks go inside quotation marks. Check this out in books of fiction. Get up now and look for conversations in stories. Do it.**

I recommend you now take a week off from writing and concentrate on reading and discussing ideas with your parents.

RECORD OF PROGRESS

Name:_____ Date:_____

Exercise **#11 HOW PEOPLE MOVE WHEN THEY TALK**

This is the best sentence I wrote this week.

_____

_____

This mistake I made this week and I will not make it next week.

_____

_____

This is the sentence that had this mistake in it.

_____

_____

This is the sentence again showing how I fixed this mistake.

_____

_____

Comments:

#12 STORY EVENTS

SKILL: ORGANIZATION

It may take you eleven days to learn that:
1. A **story is** a series of **events**
2. The **order** of these events in stories must be **logical** (make sense)
3. **You can write a story** from a list of events you've created

This is a three-part exercise:
1. Story Events One
2. Story Events Two
3. Story Events Three

STORY EVENTS ONE

PREWRITING

Days One and Two:

    You'll pick a story to read or your parent will assign one. You should take notes about the **events** in the story which can look like the example below.

                                                   (Your Name)

(Skip two spaces)

"Story Title"

(Be sure to put the story's title inside quotation marks.)

(Example events)

1. *John asks for permission to get paper route*
2. *Mother says no he's too young*
3. *John asks people and family friends how old they were when they started*
4. *They write about delivering papers*
5. *Mother reads stories and agrees*

> **Hint: Note the capitals on the items in a list.**

In your notes, it's not necessary that you write in complete sentences. **Words or phrases will do.** Be sure that you **list only events.** Don't list how the characters feel or what they want—only **what happens.**

Notice again, when I wrote the list, I used **present tense**: *John asks*. When you talk or write about what happens in a story, you should always use present tense. So, you will be writing the events in present tense just as in this example: *When Bill **sees** his mother, he **asks** if he can get a job.*

WRITING

Day Three:
You should turn the items on your list into sentences, just as I've done below:

*1. John **asks** his mother for permission to get a paper route.*
*2. His mother says **no** because he's too young.*
*3. John **visits** lots of people and asks about when they had their first paper route.*
*4. John has them **write** their stories so that he can show them to his mother.*
*5. John's mother reads the stories and **agrees** that John can have a paper route.*

STORY EVENTS TWO

Day Four:
In "Story Events One" you listed the events in a selected story. Think of some events for a story you'll be writing. Then you'll have to create a character.

You should decide what kind of person the reader of your story will be. You should create a character to be like that reader. Identify the type of person your reader will be and put this at the top of the page. It could look like this example:

> *(Your Name)*
>
> *READER*
> *Girl*
> *Seventh grade*
> *Likes to keep busy*
> *Is ambitious*
> *Wants to start saving money so she can go to college to learn to be a pig farmer.*

Hint: Pig farmers have good lives.

You should create a **list of the characteristics** for your character:

A. Age:_____ B. Boy or girl: _____

C. Type of person: _____

_____

D. Likes to do: _____

_____

E. What he or she likes to talk about: _____

2. Your next step will be to **create a problem** your character will have. This can be something your character wants or something that your character has to do that's hard to do. This part of your exercise should be at least one long paragraph. Be sure your parent has seen your work on day four before you start on day five work.

Days Five and Six:

3. You're now ready to list the **events** in your story. You should number these events in the order they are to occur. Just as in "Story Events One," the items in your list **don't have to be in sentences.**

After your parent has read your list, you should turn the items into sentences.

STORY EVENTS THREE

Day Seven:

You'll find it's easy to write a story from the series of events that you wrote in list form for "Story Events Two."

It may help you to go back and read through the exercise, "A Very Short Story."

You'll have to:
1. **Create a place** for your story
2. **Create a character** your reader will like
   (*Now comes the list of events*)
3. Give this character **a problem**
4. Have your character **solve this problem**

Hint: The problems must always be important to the characters

Identify these steps on your paper as is done on the lines below:

One or two words will be enough to identify each.

1. **Place:** _____

2. **Character:** _____

3. **Problem:** _____

4. **The Solution:** _____

Days Eight through Eleven:

It should take you one day to write about each of the above four points. This means that you'll:

- Write about the **place** on day **eight**

- Create the **character** on day **nine**

- Set up the **problem** on day **ten**

- Have the character **solve the problem** on day **eleven**.

Note: These pieces of your story should look just like all stories do. They should **not** be on five pieces of paper but should be together.

If you want to work faster than this outline suggests, great. Do it. There may be no need to follow the days in these exercises. If you like what you're doing and your parent thinks you're doing well and tells you that it's okay to do them faster, work as fast as you can, but be sure you still do as good a job as you can.

But, don't think that you're doing a good job just because you write quickly. Writing well is very hard and does take a lot of time. Some authors work for hours and end up with just one sentence they like. It will really help your writing if you examine every sentence carefully. Rewrite those that do not do *exactly* what you want them to do. Writing, like anything else that can be beautiful, takes great patience.

> **Hint: Remember how to write with detail? If not, read through lesson two again.**

I recommend you now take a week off from writing and concentrate on reading and discussing ideas with your parents.

RECORD OF PROGRESS

Name:_____ Date:_____

Exercise *#12* **STORY EVENTS**

This is the best sentence I wrote this week.

_____

_____

This mistake I made this week and I will not make it next week.

_____

_____

This is the sentence that had this mistake in it.

_____

_____

This is the sentence again showing how I fixed this mistake.

_____

_____

Comments:

#13 TELL A STORY

SKILL: CREATION

It may take you just a few days to learn to:
1. Plan the telling of an event
2. Supply the details to the parts of the event
3. Tell the parts of the event in the order in which they happen
4. Keep the same point of view as you turn the events into a story

PREWRITING

Day One:

In this exercise you'll become a real author. The author of a story is a person who knows something or makes something up and tells it to another person. You won't find this hard to do, but there are some rules a good author must follow.

First, a few ideas about the "voice" of a storyteller. This voice is called the **narrative voice,** but the author is *not* the voice that speaks to the reader. The author creates a voice to talk to the reader. It is this voice which tells the story. The author writes the story on the page, but the "teller" of the story is the **narrative voice** who says the words to the reader. If this isn't clear, read this paragraph again.

This voice can even be **a character** in the story. (Ask your parent to talk about this idea. It can get complicated, and it's very important that you understand it.)

When the narrative voice is a character in the story, that means that the **voice is a person in the story**, and the voice sounds like this:

> *I saw the old man in the window of the vacant house. I was not a bit scared. I ran home because I had a lot of chores to do.*

The *I* in this example is both the *narrative voice* **and** a character in the story. If this is not clear to you, ask your parent to go over it again. You must understand this idea.

Hint: Proofread your work by reading what you have written slowly and out loud.

When the **narrative voice is not a character** in the story but is what is called **a non-character**, then the **voice is not part of the story**. This kind of voice sounds like it's standing outside of the story looking in and telling the reader what happens to the people in the story. This **non-character voice** sounds like this:

The young girl was not scared when she saw the old man in the window of the vacant house. She ran home because she had a lot of chores to do.

What I want you to understand is that there are **two narrative voices** in storytelling.

1. There is the **voice who is a character** in the story and tells the reader what happens.

2. There is the **voice who is outside the story** and watches the characters in the story and tells the reader what happens.

An author must be careful not to mix up these two narrative voices in one story.

REVIEW
A. If you were to use **a narrative voice which is part of the story**, your story would sound like the storyteller **is a character** in the action of the story.

B. If you were to use a **narrative voice which is not a part of the story**, your story would sound like the storyteller is telling something that had **happened to someone else.**

You have a chance to practice (**A**), a **first person voice**—as if you were a **character**.

You'll write a story in which you'll create **a voice which is part of the action**. You'll use the word *I* in this story. This is called **first person.** This means you'll tell the story **as if it happened to you**.

There are now **six steps** to organizing the writing of a story:

1. Select a **voice**
2. Select **a time**
3. Select **a place**
4. List a **group of events** in which there is a problem and a solution
5. Decide on **the order** of the telling of the events
6. **Describe** the events

We can do this list of steps together. Next time you can do them by yourself. Let's write the story about the person who has all the chores to do.

Hint: Commas separate place names in an address.

---

1. We'll use **first person**; this means the voice in the story will be **part of the action**. The story will sound as if it happened to the writer. We'll use the word, *I*. It'll read like this:

   I saw *the man in the window.*

2. We must select a **time**. Let's tell this story as if it has already happened—as if it happened in the past. This is called *past tense*. It'll read like this:

   I saw the old man in the window **last night**.

3. Let's **place** the story in your town. We can place it anywhere we want to, but you know your town pretty well.

4. We must **list the events** of our story. Let's do this together:

   A. ***I was walking home*** *from my friend's house just as the sun was setting.*
   B. *I had to* **walk past the old Finster house** *on the hill.*
   C. *I* **kept my eyes on the house** *as I walked past.*
   D. *I saw* **a movement** *in one of the windows.*
   E. *I was sure I saw a person in the window.*
   F. *I remembered Old Man* **Finster had moved** *two years ago.*
   G. *I knew no one had moved in because the* **"For Sale" sign was still** *out by the road.*
   H. ***I ran on home*** *because I had a lot of chores to do*

5. I listed the events of the story in the **order in which they happen**. This is called **chronological** order. This means logical time. This means that we must tell the first thing that happens first, the second thing that happens second, and so on.

6. We must now **describe the events**. When we do this, we'll have written the story. We'll need to make at least one paragraph out of each of the events we've listed.

It would be good practice for you to make your paragraphs between four and eight sentences long. (That's a lot of writing, but you should be liking it by now.) The main ideas for these paragraphs will be the items in the list.

If you look back, you'll see the first item in our list was (A.) *Walking home at sundown.* We have to turn this first item into a paragraph. We must describe what the walk was like. We could talk about the time of year. How about late in October? We could talk about what the weather was like. Windy? Rain clouds? We could describe the trees along the roadside and the country road—how lonely it was and getting darker.

> **Hint: Keep person and tense consistent.**

There are lots of things we could tell about that walk home. There are lots of things we could tell about each of the items on the list. This is what an author does, fills in the details. This is your job. You're to make a decision about what to tell for each of the items on the list.

The next step is to turn these items into sentences. When that's done, you'll have quite a long and detailed story.

I'll give you a model for the first paragraph or so. Then you'll have to do the other six items by yourself.

The Long Walk Home

I remember the walk home that night very well. It was late in October, near the end of the month, I think. It had been a cold day, and there were dark clouds piling up in the west. They had hidden the setting sun and were moving quickly over me, for there was a strong wind blowing. The dark and bare trees along the lonely road creaked and moaned as they were blown this way and that. Their branches seemed to reach and clutch at me like old and thin hands.

As I hurried along, I noticed that the lights of my friend's house had disappeared around the bend, and the other few houses on that long, gravel road were dark.

Since we wrote this first paragraph together, you should be able to use it for your story.

WRITING

Day Two to the End of the Story:
You should be able to write one event each day. This means this story should take you at least nine days to write. Your job is to finish the story. You must keep using the same voice (**person**) and time (**tense**). We started the story in **first person** and **past tense**. Use them.

| Hint: Check your paper for clichés |

I recommend you now take a week off from writing and concentrate on reading and discussing ideas with your parents.

RECORD OF PROGRESS

Name:_____ Date:_____

Exercise #13 TELL A STORY

This is the best sentence I wrote this week.

_____

_____

This mistake I made this week and I will not make it next week.

_____

_____

This is the sentence that had this mistake in it.

_____

_____

This is the sentence again showing how I fixed this mistake.

_____

_____

Comments:

#14 LIKING THE CHARACTER

SKILL: CREATION

It may take you four days to learn that:
1. Readers like only some of the characters in stories
2. You can create characters that your readers will like

PREWRITING

Days One and Two:

You've liked some characters in stories and have wanted them to be successful in what they wanted to do. Other characters you've not liked and have wanted them to fail. Different readers like different characters. A character whom you like your mother or your father might not like. All the kids your age might not like the same characters in a story.

Authors know this, and one of the first things an author has to do is figure out who'll be reading the story. One way a writer makes the characters so that the readers will like them is to make them similar to the expected readers. Notice that most of the characters in the books you like to read are about people near your age.

Characters in stories:
1. Are about the **same age** as the readers
2. **Like** the **same** objects (toys or tools)
3. Have the **same problems**
4. Have the **same fears**
5. Like to **do the same** things the readers like doing

Soon you'll create a character for a story you'll be sure kids your age would like. You should use the five items in the above list to do this. You should have at least two sentences in your writing for each item on the list.

When you write about the age of your character, you can also talk about:

1. What **activities** the character enjoys
2. How **big** the character is
3. If the character **acts his or her age**

A run-on (comma splice) is two sentences connected by a comma, this is one. Avoid.

WRITING

Days Three and Four:

Your parent will assign a story for you to read and ask you to pick out and describe the main character. You should use the above list to do this. There may not be as much information in the story as there is in your list, but that won't be a problem.

Write a sentence at the end of your listing about whether the character is or is not like the kids you know who are about your age. When you're done with the listing, ask your parent to read over what you've written. Set your paper up like this example:

(Your Name)

Story Title
(Be sure to use quote marks around the name of any story.)

Author's Name

The Main Character

1. The activities the character enjoys:

   A _____

   B _____

   C _____

2. How big and how old the character is: _____
   _____

3. How the character acts or what the character does: _____
   _____

Page number bottom center

Hint: Check to be sure you used full sentences.

I recommend you now take a week off from writing and concentrate on reading and discussing ideas with your parents.

RECORD OF PROGRESS

Name:_____ Date:_____

Exercise *#14* LIKING THE CHARACTER

This is the best sentence I wrote this week.

_____

_____

This mistake I made this week and I will not make it next week.

_____

_____

This is the sentence that had this mistake in it.

_____

_____

This is the sentence again showing how I fixed this mistake.

_____

_____

Comments:

PROBLEMS I HAVE SOLVED
THIS SECOND SEMESTER

1. _____

   _____

2. _____

   _____

3. _____

   _____

4. _____

   _____

5. _____

   _____

6. _____

   _____

7. _____

   _____

8. _____

   _____

9. _____

   _____

SECOND SEMESTER REPORT
on
WRITING SKILLS MASTERY

THIRD LEVEL WRITING EXERCISES

Student Name:_____ Grade:_____

Skills   Needs
Mastered   Experience

Exercise 7: Furniture
Skill Area: Organization

_____   _____   1. Examining a number of objects
_____   _____   2. Organizing objects so their placement can be understood

Exercise 8: Out the Window
Skill Area: Description

_____   _____   1. Understanding that all people don't see the same things
_____   _____   2. Organizing what is seen
_____   _____   3. Establishing a character's position by telling what that character can see

Exercise 9: A Very Short Story
Skill Area: Creation

_____   _____   1. Planning a very short story
_____   _____   2. Writing the parts of a very short story
_____   _____   3. Putting story parts together

Exercise 10. My Room
Skill Area: Description

_____   _____   1. Understanding that the world is an organized place
_____   _____   2. Realizing the need to understand organization
_____   _____   3. Describing something in an organized way

Skills   Needs
Mastered   Experience

Exercise 11: How People Move When They Talk
Skill Area: Description

_____   _____   1. Punctuating dialogue
_____   _____   2. Describing characters' dialogue
_____   _____   3. Writing so that characters move as they talk

Exercise 12: Story Events
Skill Area: Organization

_____   _____   1. Understanding that a story is a series of events
_____   _____   2. Understanding that the order of events is logical
_____   _____   3. Writing a series of events for a story
_____   _____   4. Creating a story from a series of events you have listed

Exercise 13: Tell a Story
Skill Area: Creation

_____   _____   1. Planning the telling of an event
_____   _____   2. Supplying the details to the event
_____   _____   3. Telling the parts of the event in order
_____   _____   4. Maintaining a point of view

Exercise 14: Liking the Character
Skill Area: Creation

_____   _____   1. Understanding that all characters in stories are not liked by all readers
_____   _____   2. Creating characters who will be liked by your readers

COMMON PROBLEMS

WITH DEFINITIONS * RULES * EXAMPLES

AMBIGUITY

A statement may be taken in two ways.

1. *She saw the man walking down the street.*

   This can mean either:

   A. *She saw the man when she was walking down the street;* or,
   B. *She saw the man when he was walking down the street.*

2. The use of pronouns *it, she, they, them* that do not have clear antecedents (what they refer to) can create ambiguous sentences:

   Bill looked at the coach when <u>he</u> got the money.

   This can mean either:

   A. *When Bill got the money he looked at the coach;* or,
   B. *Bill looked at him when the coach got the money.*

APOSTROPHE

An apostrophe (') is a mark used to indicate possession or contraction.

Rules:

1. To form the possessive case (who owns it) of a singular noun (one person or thing), add an apostrophe and an *s*.

   Example: *the girl's coat   Bill's ball   the car's tire*

2. To form the possessive case of a plural noun (two or more people or things) ending in *s*, add only the apostrophe.

   Example: *the boys' car   the cars' headlights*

3. Do not use an apostrophe for: *his, hers, its, ours, yours, theirs, whose.*

   Example: *The car was theirs.   The school must teach its students.*

4. Indefinite pronouns: (could be anyone) *one, everyone, everybody,* require an apostrophe and an *s* to show possession.

> Example: *One's* car is important.   That must be *somebody's* bat.

5. An apostrophe shows where letters have been omitted in a contraction (making one word out of two).

> Example: *can't* for cannot   *don't* for do not
> *we've* for we have   *doesn't* for does not

Note that the apostrophe goes in the word where the letter or letters are omitted.

AWKWARD WRITING

Awkward writing is rough and clumsy. It can be confusing to the reader and make the meaning unclear. Many times just the changing of the placement of a word or the changing of a word will clear up the awkwardness.

If you read your work out loud or have someone else read to it to you and then to listen to what you are saying, you can catch the awkwardness. Remember that you have to read loud enough to hear your own voice.

1. *Each of you kids will have to bring each day each of the following things: pen, pencil and paper.*

   This should be rewritten to read:

   Each day bring pens, pencils and paper.

2. *The bird flew down near the ground, and having done this, began looking for bugs or worms because it was easier to see them down low than it had been when it was flying high in the sky.*

   There are many problems with that sentence. To get rid of its awkwardness, it could be rewritten to read: *The bird, looking for food, swooped low.*

   Keep in mind that the point of your writing is for you to give your readers information. The simplest way to do this may be the best way.

CLICHÉ

All of us like to use expressions we've heard or read. Many times you'll use expressions in your writing that you won't realize have been used so many times before that they no longer are fresh and exciting for your readers. The best way to avoid this is to read your work aloud and listen for familiar phrases. Omit them. Some examples below:

round as a dollar	*pretty as a picture*	*tall as a tree*
fell flat on his face	*he stopped in his tracks*	*stone cold dead*
snapped back to reality	*graceful as a swan*	*stiff as a board*
limber as a willow	*he roared like a lion*	*white as a sheet*

Usually the first expressions young writers think of when they write will be clichés. If you think you've heard of an expression before, don't use it.

COMMAS

You can solve most of your comma problems if you read your work out loud and listen to where your voice drops in each sentence. There is where a comma goes. This will work for about 95% of comma placement. This works because commas are needed and used to make clear the meaning in writing. They indicate a pause or a separation of ideas.

Rules:

1. To separate place names—as in an address, dates, or items in a series
2. To set off introductory or concluding expressions
3. To make clear the parts of a compound sentence
4. To set off transitional or non-restrictive words or expressions in a sentence

Examples:

1. *During the day on May 3, 1989, I began to study.*

   I had courses in English, math and geography at a little school in Ann Arbor, Michigan.

   The parts of the date should be separated by commas, and the courses in this sentence which come in a list should be separated by commas. You have a choice of whether to put a comma before the *and* just prior to the last item on a list.

2. *After the bad showing on the test, Bill felt he had to study more than he had.*

   The introduction—*After the bad showing on the test*—to the central idea of this sentence—*Bill felt he had to study more*—is set off from this central idea by a comma.

3. *Bill went to class to study for the test, and I went to the snack bar to feed the inner beast.*

There are two complete ideas here: 1) *Bill went to study*; and, 2) *I went to eat*. These two ideas can be joined in a compound (two or more things put together) sentence if there is a conjunction (*and*, *but*, *though*) between them and they are separated by a comma. Notice where the comma is placed in the example below.

4. *Bob, who didn't really care, made only five points on the test.*

The central idea of this fourth sentence is that Bob made only five points on the test. The information given that he didn't care is interesting but not essential to the understanding of the main idea of the sentence. The commas indicate that the words between them are not essential to the meaning of the sentence.

COMMA SPLICE

A comma splice is when the two halves of a compound sentence are joined/separated by a comma.

Example:

Bill had to take the test over again, he felt sorry he would miss the party.

A comma splice can be avoided by writing this sentence in one of the five following ways.

1. *Bill had to take the test over again and felt sorry he would miss the party.*

2. *Bill had to take the test over again; he felt sorry he would miss the party.*

3. *Bill had to take the test over again, and he felt sorry he would miss the party.*

4. *Bill had to take the test over again: he felt sorry he would miss the party.*

5. *Bill had to take the test over again. He felt sorry he would miss the party.*

Notice that the punctuation of each of the above examples gives the reader a different idea about Bill and how he felt.

DIALOGUE STRUCTURE and PUNCTUATION

Dialogue is conversation between two or more people. When shown in writing, it refers to the speech or thoughts of characters.

Rules:

Dialogue can occur either in the body of the writing, but usually there is a separate line for each new speaker.

Examples:

1.   *John took his test paper from the teacher and said to him, "This looks like we will get to know each other well." The teacher looked surprised and said with a smile, "I hope so."*

2.   *John took his test paper from the teacher and said to him, "This looks like you and I will get to know each other well."*
     The teacher looked surprised and said with a smile, "I hope so."

3.   *John took his test paper from the teacher and thought, "This looks like I'll get to know this old man well this year." The teacher looked surprised—almost as if he had read John's mind—and thought, "I hope so."*

DICK AND JANE WRITING:

Writing is called this because of the way Dick and Jane books are written. *See Dick. See Jane. See Dick and Jane run. They are running to town.* This could be rewritten to read: *Look, Dick and Jane are running to town.*

FLOWERY WRITING

You will use flowery writing when you want to impress your readers with how many good words you can use to express ideas. This results in the words used becoming more important than the ideas presented.

Rule: A general rule that should apply is: What you say should be put simply.

Example:

The red and fiery sun slowly settled into the distant hills like some great, billowing sailing ship sinking beyond the horizon. It cast its pink and violet flags along the tops of the clouds where they waved briefly before this ship of light slid beneath the waves of darkness and cast us all, there on the beach, into night.

This is so flowery that it is hard to read without laughing.

It should be rewritten to read:

As the sun set, we remained on the beach, gazing at the darkening sky.

MODIFIER (dangling)

This means that there is nothing for the modifier to modify in the sentence.

> Examples: *Getting up, my arms felt tired. (How did the arms get up all by themselves?)*

This should read: *When I got up my arms felt tired.*

Coming down the street, my feet wanted to turn into the park. (Again, how did the feet do this?)

This should read: *Coming down the street, I felt as if my feet wanted to turn toward the park.*

Being almost asleep, the accident made me jump. It is clear the accident could not have been asleep.

This should read: *I was almost asleep and the accident made me jump.*

OMITTED WORDS

Most of us leave words out of sentences, or leave the endings off of words. You can solve this problem if you read your work out loud and slowly. You must do this slowly enough that you can catch every syllable. I have had adult students get angry after I have asked them to read what they have written for the fifth or sixth time before they recognized what they had left out.

PARAGRAPH

A paragraph is a sentence or a group of sentences developing one idea or topic.

Rules:

In nonfiction writing, a paragraph consists of a topic sentence which is supported by other sentences giving additional details. A good rule is: A paragraph in this kind of writing should have at least four supportive sentences, making at least five sentences for every paragraph.

Example:

TOPIC SENTENCE: One sentence that introduces the reader to the main idea of the paragraph.

PARAGRAPH DEVELOPMENT: May be made by facts, examples, incidents, comparison, contrast, definition, reasons (in the form of arguments) or combination.

QUOTATION MARKS

Quotation marks are used to indicate exact words or thoughts and to indicate short works and chapters of long works.

Rule:

1. You should put in quotation marks the direct quotation of a person's words. When you use other marks of punctuation with quotation marks: 1) you should put commas and periods inside the quotation marks; and, 2) put other punctuation marks inside the quotation marks if they are part of the quotation; if they are not part of the quotation, you should put them outside of the quotation marks.

Example:

The salesman said, "This is the gum all the kids are chewing."

2. Put in quotation marks the titles of chapters, articles, other parts of books or magazines, short poems, short stories and songs.

Example:

In this magazine there were two things I really liked: "The Wind Blows Free" and "Flowers," the poems by the young girl.

REDUNDANCY

Redundancy means using different words to say the same thing. The writer does not gain by this, only confuses and bores the reader.

Examples:

I, myself, feel it is true.
It is plain and clear to see.
Today, in the world, there is not room for lack of care for the ecology.

This is an easy mistake to make, and it will take conscious thought for you to avoid this problem. Use care when you are proofreading your work.

RHYMING

The man was feeling really *well* until he *fell*. The rhyming words will ring bells in the reader's mind and detract from what the writer wants the reader to think about.

Example:

The sentence should be re-written to read: *The man was feeling really well until he stumbled on the driveway and slid under the greasy truck.*

SENTENCE

RUN-ON: This is the combining of two or more sentences as if they were one.

Example:

Bill saw that the fish was too small he put it back in the lake and then put a fresh worm on his hook. (This sentence needs to be broken into two sentences by putting a period between *small* and *he*. It could also be correct with a semicolon between *small* and *he*.)

FRAGMENT: This is part of a sentence which lacks a subject or a verb or both.

Check your sentences to make sure they have both subjects and verbs. But, Fragments can be powerful if used correctly:

Example:

When Janet reached her door she found it was partly open. A burglar! Someone had been in her house and had left the door open.

SUBJECT-VERB AGREEMENT (number)

Closely related words have matching forms, and, when the forms match, they agree. Subjects and their verbs agree if they both are singular or both are plural.

Rules: Singular subjects require singular verbs, and plural subjects require plural verbs.

Examples:

Singular: *car, man, that, she, he, it*   Singular: *The heater was good.*
The heater works well.

Plural: *cars, men, those, women, they*   Plural: *The heaters were good.*
The heaters work well.

Most nouns form their plural by adding the letter *s*, as in *bats* and *cats*. The clue is the final *s*.

It is just the opposite with most verbs. A verb ending in *s* is usually singular, as in *puts, yells, is* and *was*.

Most verbs not ending in *s* are plural, as in *they put, they yell*. The exceptions are verbs used with *I* and singular *you*: *I put, you put*.

TENSE ERROR

Tense errors occur when writers mix past and present tenses and do not have justification for changing from one to the other.

Rules.

1. **Present tense** is used to describe actions that are taking place at the time of the telling of the event.

   Example: *John is in the house. Mr. Jones lives there.*

2. **Past tense** is used to describe actions that have already happened.

   Example: *John was in the house. Mr. Jones lived there.*

3. **Future tense** is used to describe actions that will happen.

   Example: *John will be in the house. Mr. Jones will live there.*

National Writing Institute Order Form

		Qty.	Total
❏	*Writing Strands* **Level 1** Oral work for ages 3-8	$14.95 ea. ____	_____
❏	*Writing Strands* **Level 2** About 7 years old	$18.95 ea. ____	_____
❏	*Writing Strands* **Level 3** Starting program ages 8-12	$18.95 ea. ____	_____
❏	*Writing Strands* **Level 4** Any age after Level 3 or starting program at age 13 or 14	$18.95 ea. ____	_____
❏	*Writing Strands* **Level 5** Any age after Level 4 or starting program at age 15 or 16	$20.95 ea. ____	_____
❏	*Writing Strands* **Level 6** 17 or any age after Level 5	$20.95 ea. ____	_____
❏	*Writing Strands* **Level 7** 18 or any age after Level 6	$22.95 ea. ____	_____
❏	*Writing Exposition* Senior high school and after Level 7	$22.95 ea. ____	_____
❏	*Creating Fiction* Senior high school and after Level 7	$22.95 ea. ____	_____
❏	*Evaluating Writing* Parents' manual for all levels of *Writing Strands*	$19.95 ea. ____	_____
❏	*Reading Strands* Parents' manual for story and book interpretation, all grades	$22.95 ea. ____	_____
❏	*Communication and Interpersonal Relationships* Communication manners (teens)	$17.95 ea. ____	_____
❏	*Dragonslaying Is for Dreamers* - **package** 1st novel in *Dragonslaying* trilogy (early teens) and parents' manual for analyzing the novel.	$18.95 ea. ____	_____
❏	*Dragonslaying Is for Dreamers* - **novel only**	$9.95 ea. ____	_____
❏	*Axel Meets the Blue Men* 2nd novel in *Dragonslaying* trilogy (teens)	$9.95 ea. ____	_____
❏	*Axel's Challenge* Final novel in *Dragonslaying* trilogy(teens)	$9.95 ea. ____	_____
❏	*Dragonslaying* **trilogy** All three novels in series	$25.00 set ____	_____

SUBTOTAL: _____

Texas residents add **7.75%** sales tax _____

U.S. Shipping:
 $2.00 per book (**$4.00 Minimum**)................... _____

Outside U.S. Shipping:
 $4.00 per book (**$8.00 Minimum**)................... _____

TOTAL U.S. FUNDS:

CHECK or MONEY ORDER........................... _____

CREDIT CARD.. _____

Account Number

Expiration date: Month ☐☐   Year ☐☐

_____
Signature

(PLEASE PRINT) We ship U.P.S. to the 48 states, so please no P.O. #.

Name: _____

Street: _____

City: _____

State: _____ Zip: _____

Phone: (_____)_____

E-Mail (if available) _____

SHIPPING INFORMATION
Continental US : We ship via UPS ground service. Most customers will receive their orders within 10 business days.

Alaska, Hawaii, US Military addresses and US territories: We ship via US Priority Mail. Orders generally arrive within 2 weeks.

Canada: We ship via Air Mail. Most customers receive orders within 2 weeks.

Other international destinations: We generally ship via Air Mail. Delivery times vary.

RETURNS
Our books are guaranteed to please you. If they do not, return them within 30 days and we'll refund the full purchase price.

PRIVACY
We respect your privacy. We will not sell, rent or trade your personal information.

INQUIRIES AND ORDERS:
Phone:	(800) 688-5375 TOLLFREE
Fax:	(888) 663-7855 TOLLFREE
Write:	**National Writing Institute** 624 W. University #248 Denton, TX 76201-1889
E-mail:	info@writingstrands.com
Website:	www.writingstrands.com

NEW ADDRESS